Snowboard Baby

Written by
Simmons Ingenthrone

Illustrated by
Nadia Ronquillo

Snowboard Baby
© 2024 by Simmons Ingenthrone

Written by Simmons Ingenthrone
Illustrated by Nadia Ronquillo

ISBN: 979-8-9906690-0-0

To Nolan and Eva our baby snowboarders.

for all parents and children willing to try new things together.

Mom and Dad love to snowboard. When they had a baby, they knew that someday their baby would learn to snowboard too.

04

They put their heads together and came up with a great idea.

**If baby can stand,
baby can stand on a board...
right?**

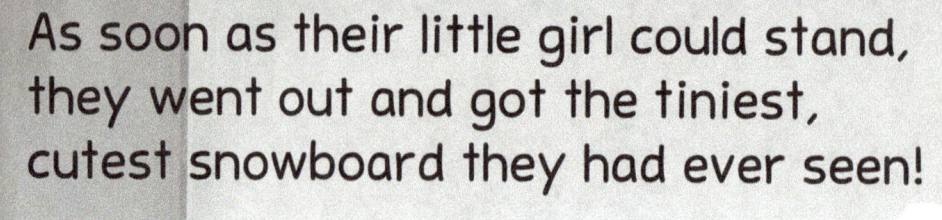

As soon as their little girl could stand, they went out and got the tiniest, cutest snowboard they had ever seen!

Once they got home,
baby couldn't wait to play with it.

They put on her snow boots and helmet, and when she was comfortable, they put baby on the board and strapped in her feet.

Baby was happy!

But there was a problem.... It was the middle of summer. No snow.

Mom said,
"What can we do here
at home?"

Dad had an idea.
"Let's tie something to the
board and pull her around
the house."

Mom got a dog leash, then hooked it to
one of the bindings.

10

Baby was ready!

On the carpet, baby was able to easily glide around. When they went over a hard floor, they wrapped a towel around the bottom of the board to help her slide (and keep the board from scratching the floor)

Baby fell on her butt a few times and started to get upset, so they attached a little pillow to her for some cushion.

As they were practicing, she fell some more, and started to cry. "No worries honey. You tried so hard! We'll practice more later." Mom and Dad were always very loving and patient.

They practiced every chance they got.

In the house,

outside in the yard,

and at the park.

Some days, baby did not want to practice.
"That's ok honey, no worries. We'll try again later."

15

Soon it was winter. There was finally snow on the ground! Mom and dad bundled baby up in her snow gear, grabbed her helmet and board, and went out into the yard.

They let baby play for a while, then when she was ready, put her on her board. Dad held the dog leash and slowly towed her around.

At first, Mom held her hand while pulling the leash, then let go so baby could try to balance on her own.

Sometimes baby's gloves fell off.

Sometimes baby face planted.

Sometimes baby would cry.

No matter what, Mom and Dad were always loving and patient.

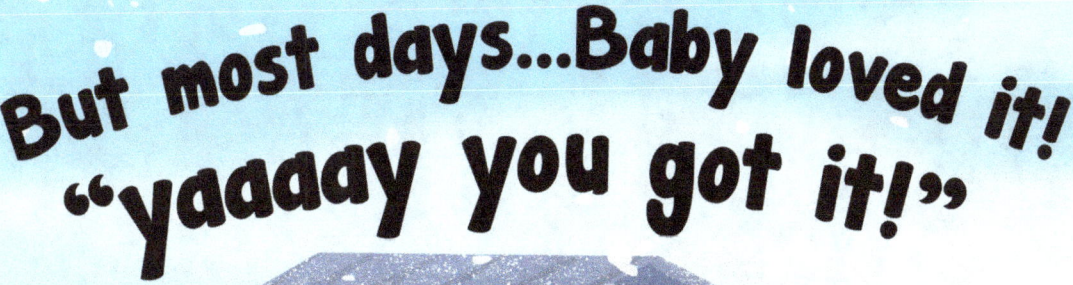

But most days...Baby loved it!
"yaaaay you got it!"

Mom and Dad would yell
(while also trying to catch their
breath). It was so much fun!

21

Now it was time for the mountain.

The big day was here!

At the ski resort, they showed baby
the BIG mountain trails, and the learning area
where they were going to practice.

Everyone was very excited!

When baby was comfortable, they got her on her board and guided her slowly down the learning hill, just like they had practiced at home. Almost everyone stopped to watch.

Soon, baby was a toddler. She now had a special harness and was ready for the BIG mountain.
This was the day Mom and Dad had been waiting for.

They rode the gondola all the way to the very
top of the mountain.

As they made their way down, there was lots of falling, laughing, taking breaks, and a little crying, but they did it together.

Baby was snowboarding!

When they got to the bottom, everyone was exhausted.

28

They went to the lodge to rest
and have some snacks.

After they finished eating, baby looked at them and said,

"Can we go again?"

"YAAAAAAAAAAAAAY!"

About the Author

Simmons is a Colorado native, wife, and mother to 2 kids. Her and her husband Sal live in the suburbs of Denver, and love to snowboard. After some trial and error, they found a unique way to introduce their babies to snowboarding from the comfort of their own home. When they realized that what they were doing worked, they decided to create a Youtube video and this children's book so they could share their idea with other families. Go to babycandoit.com for more info

About the Illustrator

Nadia Ronquillo is a children's book illustrator, visual development artist, and content creator from Ecuador. She majored in Graphic Design and Audiovisual Production. Right away, she started freelancing as a children's book illustrator and collaborating remotely as a visual development artist. For the past ten years, she has been helping self-published authors go from manuscript to PDF-ready for publication. For projects, please visit her website at www.nadiaronquilloart.com.